DIGGING UP THE PAST

MUMMIES
SECRETS OF THE DEAD

Richard Raleigh

HIGH
interest
books

Children's Press®
A Division of Scholastic Inc.
New York / Toronto / London / Auckland / Sydney
Mexico City / New Delhi / Hong Kong
Danbury, Connecticut

Book Design: Christopher Logan and Erica Clendening
Contributing Editor: Kevin Somers

Library of Congress Cataloging-in-Publication Data

Raleigh, Richard.
    Mummies : secrets of the dead / Richard Raleigh.
    p. cm. — (Digging up the past)
    Includes index.
    ISBN 0-516-25596-7 (lib. bdg.) — ISBN 0-516-25094-9 (pbk.)
    1. Mummies — Juvenile literature. I. Title. II. Digging up the past (Children's
Press)

GN293.R35 2005
393'.3 — dc22

                                              2004030081

1 2 3 4 5 6 7 8 9 10 R 14 13 12 11 10 09 08 07 06 05

CONTENTS

Conditions such as extreme heat and dry air can prevent a body from decaying. This makes a desert such as the Sahara (above) the perfect place for a body to naturally mummify.

Introduction

You are with a tour group in the vast Sahara Desert in Egypt. You are visiting the ancient pyramids. Suddenly, a terrible sandstorm begins. It soon turns the desert as black as night. As you stumble around in the dark, you become separated from your group.

Trying to find the others, you cough and choke on the swirling sand. Suddenly, something brushes against your leg. You bend down to look. You are shocked to see several thin, bony fingers reaching out from the sand!

You call for help and immediately start to dig up your discovery. What you find sends chills down your spine. You uncover a stiff, dead body. It is shriveled, as if it were dried in the sun. The body is so perfectly preserved that you can see that it was a young man—one who has been dead for about three thousand years! You have discovered a natural sand mummy.

Throughout the ages, mummies have captured our imaginations. These reminders of cultures from long ago and from faraway places fill us with wonder. How and why were mummies made? Who are these people we meet only long after they have died? What can we learn from mummies? To answer these questions, we'll need to journey back in time to the ancient past.

The mummies of a village are on display in the Asaro Caves in Papua New Guinea.

This rotting skull was found in a cemetery in Nazca, Peru. This skull is in the later stages of decay. Very little of the hair and skin remain.

CHAPTER ONE

The After-Death Experience

When a body dies, it begins to decay, or rot, and break down. This process produces terrible-smelling gases. The body can swell up to more than twice its normal size. The skin turns pale, then green, then purple, and finally black. Fluid seeps out from body openings, such as the eyes, ears, and nose. Eventually the skin slides off, the nails and hair fall off, and the body bursts.

Swarms of flies are attracted by the odor of decay. The flies lay eggs in the body openings or wounds. In a few days, the fly eggs hatch into maggots that feed on the rotting flesh. Meanwhile, flesh-eating insects and animals can also feed on the body, leaving a skeleton picked clean.

The process of body decay is a grisly one. It is not hard to imagine why people would want to keep the bodies of their loved ones preserved.

What Are Mummies?

A mummy is the body of a human or an animal that has been preserved in one of two ways. The first way a body can be preserved is accidentally, through a natural process such as freezing or drying. These types of mummies result from bodies being exposed to the elements of nature. These are called natural mummies. The other way is purposely, through a process of combining substances in order to preserve a body. When someone uses the term "mummy," we usually think of the kind purposely made by the ancient Egyptians. These types of mummies are called artificial, or man-made, mummies.

Man-Made Mummies

Many centuries ago, people probably got the idea of preserving bodies as man-made mummies after finding natural mummies. But these people probably did not understand how various substances reacted with one another to cause either body decay or preservation. It is likely that the first mummies were

This picture of the Egyptian god Anubis preparing the body of a man was painted on the wall of an ancient tomb.

made by preserving dead bodies in the same simple way that these people preserved meat and fish: by drying and salting.

Through the years, many different methods of mummification were developed. People who made mummies used a combination of drying and chemical preservation in order to keep dead bodies from decaying.

Natural Mummies

Natural mummification of human or animal remains can occur in many different ways. One way is through chemical processes, or the effect different substances have on each other. Such processes can occur in areas of wet, spongy land, such as marshes or bogs. Denmark's Tollund Man and England's Lindow Man are famous examples of preserved human remains that were found in peat marshes.

More often, natural mummies occur by the drying of remains in areas of extreme temperatures. For example, hot and dry deserts can mummify remains. Also, the very cold climates found on some high mountaintops can cause mummification in a process known as freeze-drying.

Tollund Man is a famous natural mummy found in a peat marsh. His head is on display at the Spikeborg Museum in Denmark.

ARTIFACT

Nearly a thousand man-made mummies of the Guanche (**whon**-chay) people were found in 1770 in a volcanic cave in the Canary Islands, off the northwest coast of Africa. Few of these mummies are left today. Most of them were ground up and eaten as medicine. Doctors of that time believed this medicine could remedy stomach problems.

The Inuit people of the Arctic knew that extreme cold could preserve remains. Sometimes they mummified their dead by leaving the bodies exposed in places suited for freeze-drying. Many freeze-dried Inuit mummies have been found in Greenland. It has also been discovered that the Incas of South America made sacrifices to the mountain gods by purposely freezing children in the high Andes.

Many natural mummies are the remains of people who have accidentally died. Some of the most well known include the naturally dried sand mummies of Egypt, the frozen mummy of mountain climber George Mallory who fell off the slope of Mount Everest in 1924, and Otzi the Iceman who was found on the border of Italy and Switzerland.

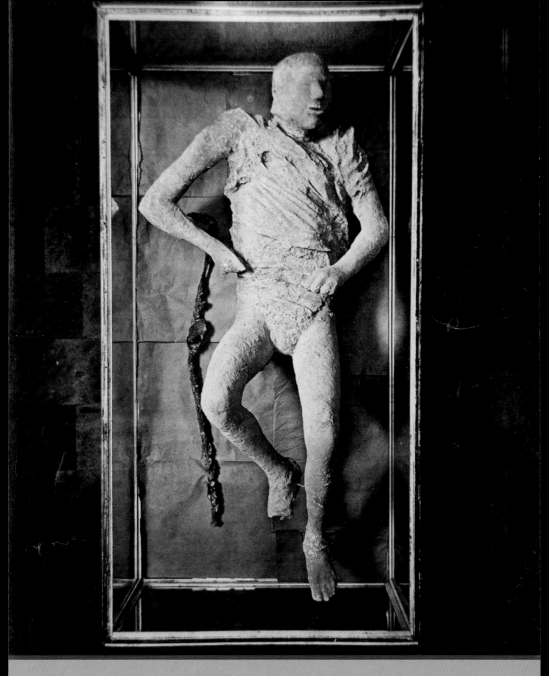

The body of this man from Pompeii was naturally mummified after being smothered in volcanic ash.

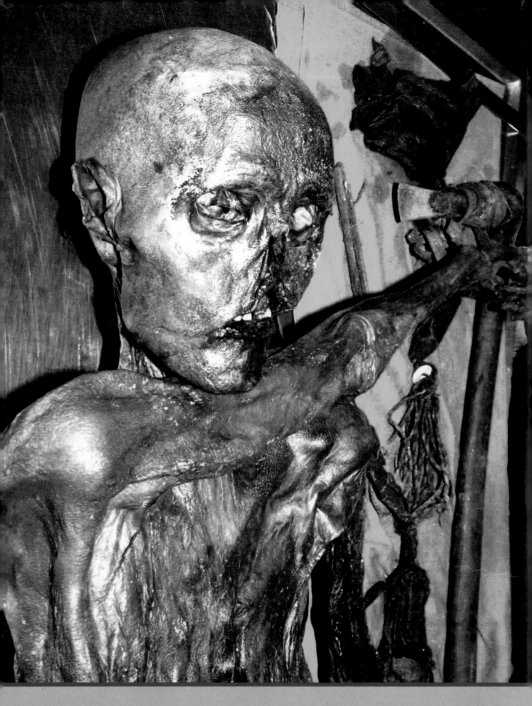

Otzi, known as the Iceman, was removed from a glacier on the Otzal Alps. He died more than five thousand years ago.

CHAPTER TWO

Unusual Mummies Around the World

Otzi the Iceman

In September 1991, two hikers in Austria's Otzal Alps found what they thought was the frozen body of a mountain climber. Bodies of other climbers had been recently found in this area. Therefore, authorities thought this body was just another unfortunate victim of a climbing accident. They had no idea that this body was over five thousand years old! It would prove to be the oldest and best-preserved natural human mummy ever found.

The hikers tried to pull the body out of the ice by tugging on its clothes. The clothing tore, destroying a part of the ancient cloth. Then they tried to pry the body from the ice and rocks with a stick. The "stick" turned out to be the mummy's ancient hunting bow. A policeman was called to the scene. He used a small jackhammer to unearth the body, but he cut into the frozen body's hip.

Finally, the body was freed with an ice pick. But its left arm was broken when the body was forced into a box for removal from the site.

Once he was removed from the ice, the iceman began to thaw and was in danger of rotting. A destructive fungus had even begun to grow on his delicate skin. Fortunately, experts refroze the body in a giant freezer.

The discovery of Otzi soon attracted the attention of many scientists. They determined that he died around 3000 B.C. He came to be known as the Iceman. Later, he was called Otzi, after the place where he was discovered.

Otzi provided scientists with a wealth of information about the Bronze Age, the time period during which he lived. His patched leather clothing, flint tools that may have been used to make fire, copper axe, and the food and medicine he carried with him taught us about life in the Bronze Age. Even the partially digested food found in his stomach gave us a clue about what people of that time ate. The Iceman is on display in the South Tyrol Museum of Archaeology in Bolanzo, Italy.

This photograph of Otzi was taken in the Otzal Alps several days after his discovery in September 1991.

ARTIFACT

Scientists recently learned that Otzi the Iceman died from an arrow wound in the back. He also had knife cuts on his forearm and his hand. These wounds suggest that he had been fighting for his life. The Iceman might be history's oldest preserved murder victim!

MUMMIES ARE EVERYWHERE

The best-preserved mummies in the world are in China. The best known of these is Lady Dai, a noblewoman who lived about twenty-two hundred years ago.

In Japan, the Buddhist Shugen-dô monks slowly starved themselves by eating such things as pine bark. They drank lacquer, a liquid used to coat and protect wood or metal, which preserved their insides. They did this to make mummies of themselves while they were still alive!

In Mexico City, Mexico, you can see the dried mummies of Wanna Watto cemetery. In Arizona in the United States, there are dried Navajo mummies. Canada is the home of the frozen mummy of Kwaday Dan Sinchi, called the North American Iceman. (For locations of mummies around the world, see the map on pages 24–25.)

The Strange Mummies of the Chinchorro

From ancient times to the present, mummification has been used as an important part of the burial rituals in many different cultures. The oldest man-made mummies in the world were found in Arica, a city located on the north coast of Chile.

This place is perfect for mummification because of its very dry climate. There are some parts of this northern region of Chile that have never gotten rain in all of recorded history!

Max Uhle, a famous German archaeologist, found the first mummies in the area near Chinchorro beach in 1917. It was learned that the earliest Chinchorro mummies dated back to about 5000 B.C. The Chinchorro people mummified everyone, from unborn infants to the elderly.

The most fascinating Chinchorro mummies were discovered more recently. In 1983, a construction crew was digging a ditch for a new water line in El Morro. A bulldozer exposed what seemed to be an ancient cemetery full of strange-looking bodies. The bodies looked like a combination of space aliens and clay puppets. Ninety-six mummies were found.

After studying the mummies, scientists confirmed that the Chinchorro mummies are perhaps the world's strangest. To make their mummies, the Chinchorro began by cutting the corpse into pieces. The arms, legs, and head were removed from the torso. The skin was then entirely peeled off and the body parts were dried. Then the skull was cut in half across the eye sockets, the brain was removed, and the empty skull was packed with various materials such as feathers and clay.

The dried skeleton was strengthened with sticks and tied back together. Later, it was covered with a thick paste made of white ash, molded to take on the shape of the former living body. Then the skin was placed back on the body and a wig of hair was added. When the original skin was unusable, the skin of a sea lion was often used.

Finally, the whole mummy was painted with a dark blue-black paint. The paint was made of a metallic substance called manganese that had been sifted from sand found on the nearby beach. When the paint dried, it gave off a beautiful black metallic gleam. The faces of the Chinchorro mummies look like clay masks.

The mummies were not immediately buried. They were first laid on the sand and tended to regularly, as if they were still alive. As time passed, the mummies were constantly repaired and touched up.

This photo shows the claylike mask of a female Chinchorro mummy. The mummy is believed to be more than seven thousand years old.

The Chinchorro people mysteriously disappeared around 1100 B.C. These beautiful, strange mummies are among the only traces of them we have left.

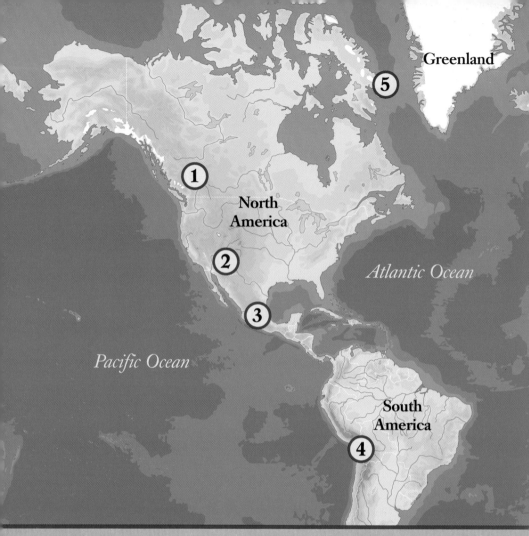

Greenland

North America

Atlantic Ocean

Pacific Ocean

South America

Mummies From Around the World

(1) **British Columbia, Canada** | Kwaday Dan Sinchi

(2) **Arizona, USA** | Navajo Mummies

(3) **Mexico City, Mexico** | Mummies of Wanna Watto Cemetery

(4) **Arica, Chile** | Mummies of the Chinchorro

(5) **Devon Island, Canada** | Franklin Expedition

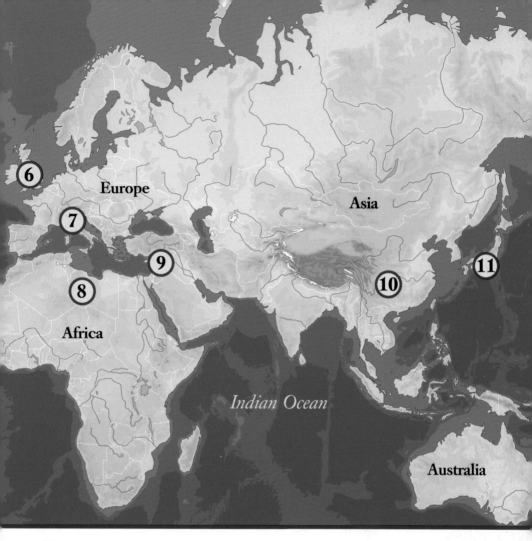

6 **Lindow Moss, Cheshire, UK** | Lindow Man

7 **Bolzano, Italy** | Otzi the Iceman

8 **Bahariya Oasis** | Bahariya Cemetery

9 **Amman, Jordan** | Mummies of the Dead Sea

10 **Changsha, China** | Lady Dai

11 **Yamagata, Japan** | Shugen-dô monks

The smooth, plastered walls of King Tutankhamen's burial chamber are painted with scenes of his funeral. The walls in the rest of his tomb are left as rough rock.

CHAPTER THREE

Tutankhamen, the Boy Pharaoh

It was November 26, 1922. The place was Egypt, in the Valley of the Kings. Howard Carter made an amazing discovery. He found the tomb of a pharaoh, or an Egyptian king, and it was almost totally untouched! After breaking through a door to the tomb, Carter was amazed to see the glint of gold everywhere!

The tomb belonged to Tutankhamen, the Boy King. King Tut, as he is commonly known today, had become pharaoh of Egypt at the young age of nine. Tut ruled until his death in 1327 B.C. when he was only eighteen.

Carter and his team wanted to make sure that everything they found was preserved and not damaged. They were so careful in their work that it took them almost three years to open King Tut's coffin. Inside they found the king's mummy, wearing a mask of solid gold. It took nearly ten years to examine and make records of all the marvelous objects they found in Tut's tomb.

ARTIFACT

A craze known as Tutmania swept the world after Carter's discovery of King Tut's tomb. This craze influenced art, fashion, and even architecture throughout the world.

The Mummy Celebrity

When King Tut's mummy was found it was not in good condition. The young pharaoh had suffered a blow to the skull. This was most likely the cause of his death. Tut's embalmers had used too much oil and resin when mummifying his body. As a result, his mummy was poorly preserved.

Tut's mummy mask is probably the most famous object ever discovered in an Egyptian tomb. It is made of solid gold and shows Tutankhamen in a royal headdress, which is what a pharaoh wore instead of a crown. The mask of Tutankhamen also has a collar decorated with falcon heads. The mask wears a false beard, and on its forehead are the heads of a cobra and a vulture.

Tut's eyes are painted to look like the eyes of Horus, the Egyptian falcon god. His headdress has strips of a precious dark blue stone called lapis lazuli and his collar and neck are ornamented with bits of glass and stone.

King Tut's solid gold mask weighs more than 22 pounds (8.2 kilograms).

Egyptian Mummification

Egyptians began mummifying their pharaohs at least forty-five hundred years ago. The practice eventually spread to include priests, wealthy people, and other members of nobility. Bodies were prepared in a place called the Beautiful House.

The Egyptians believed that Osiris, the god of the dead, was the first mummy. Legend tells us that he once lived in our world, but he was killed and torn into fourteen pieces by his evil brother Seth. Then Osiris's sister, Isis, worked with the gods Anubis and Thoth to piece Osiris back together. Anubis mummified Osiris. Then Isis breathed life into him. He was reborn in the next world as the king of the dead. The Egyptians thought they could enter the next life only if they were mummified the way they believed Osiris had been.

So the embalmers began to treat all mummies in the same manner. First, they cleaned and washed the dead body. Then they poked a metal rod upward through the nose and punctured the skull. They removed the brain by scraping it out. They slit open the lower left side of the belly and removed the intestines, the liver, the lungs, and other organs. These organs were preserved and kept in canopic jars, which were jars used to store organs. Each organ was placed in a separate jar.

Many of the canopic jars in which Egyptians stored the organs of mummies can be seen in museums such as the Egyptian Museum in Cairo (above).

The heart was usually left inside the body because the Egyptians thought it was the organ used for thinking. They also believed that the dead needed their hearts when they were judged after death by Anubis, the god who guided the dead. It was said that Anubis weighed each heart against a feather and allowed a person to enter paradise if the heart was lighter than the feather. The body was then stuffed with linen bags filled with a natural salt called natron. After the body was packed, it was then covered with about 500 pounds of natron and left for forty days to dry out. The natron drew all of the moisture from the body. This eliminated the major cause of a body's decay, which is moisture.

The dried body was then washed with alcohol to kill germs and treated with perfumed oils and spices to make the skin softer. A melted pine resin was then applied to the body. When the resin dried, the tissues of the body were entirely sealed. The body was finally wrapped in many yards of linen strips. Then it was put into a decorative wooden case and finally into a stone coffin called a sarcophagus.

This sarcophagus, from a museum in Grenoble, France, is a good example of the detailed designs and artwork on Egyptian coffins.

MORE THAN A CASE

The decorative case not only protected the embalmed body, it was believed to protect and help the person in the next life. Early Egyptian mummies were placed in a single, rectangular case. As time passed and mummification became more popular, wealthy people and nobility were put into cases that were shaped like the human body. This case was often put into a bigger one and both of these were placed into an even larger one. These multiple cases were highly decorated with colorful images and designs.

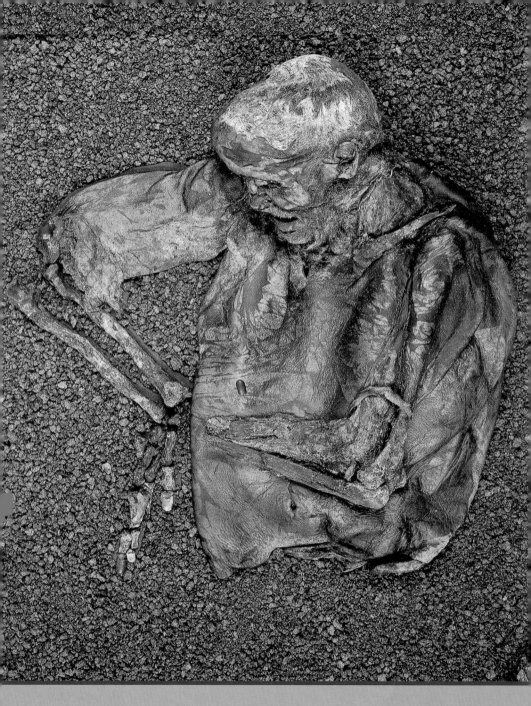

In 1984, Lindow Man, the body of an ancient natural mummy, was found in Cheshire County, England.

CHAPTER FOUR

Lindow Man, the Bog Mummy

In England in 1984, two workers named Andy Mould and Eddie Slack were loading blocks of peat onto an elevator. Peat is decayed plant matter that is often burned as a fuel. It is found in swamps and bogs. One of the workers dropped a piece of the peat, and it broke open. Inside, there was a human foot! The two workers reported their discovery to the authorities. When police arrived, they went to Lindow Moss, the bog where the workers found the foot. The police discovered a small sheet of dark human skin from a mummified body. When scientists finally arrived five days later, they cut out the large block of peat that contained the body. The scientists took it to a hospital where they tried to determine how old it was. They didn't know if it was a recent murder victim or an ancient human sacrifice, as some bodies found in bogs were said to be.

Scientific dating of the mummy determined that the unknown person, now called Lindow Man, had died sometime between 50 and 100 A.D. When scientists inspected the body closely and X-rayed it, they determined that he had been killed. His skull had been fractured from two blows from an axelike weapon. He had also been strangled, and the rope was still tightly wrapped around his neck. Two of the bones in his neck were broken. He had also been hit hard on the base of his skull. Lindow Man's throat was cut too, probably to drain his blood after death.

Lindow Man's face and body were pressed flat by the layers of peat in the bog. It was hard to imagine what he might have looked like when he was alive. However, scientists reconstructed his features. By measuring Lindow Man's upper arm bone, scientists were able to determine that he was about 5 feet 7 inches (1.7 meters) tall. He was also in good health. Because his stomach was well preserved, scientists were able to determine what his last meal was. He had eaten a snack of cereal grains and probably some burned bread.

Lindow Man was the only bearded bog mummy ever found. This photograph shows his well-preserved facial hair.

Scientists have learned much about the Lindow Man, but many questions remain unanswered, such as why was he murdered so violently?

A Human Sacrifice

Scientists have varying ideas about the death of the Lindow Man. Many believe Lindow Man was the victim of a human sacrifice during the ancient festival of Beltain, which was celebrated on May 1. That was the time when the ancient people called the Celts made sacrifices to insure a good summer crop. One of the rituals for selecting the person to be sacrificed was the use of a small cake called a bannock to draw lots. Pieces of bannock were put into a sack, including one burnt piece. The person who picked the burnt piece became the sacrifice.

A NOBLE SACRIFICE

Other bodies have been found in bogs in Denmark and in England, yet Lindow Man was unlike the others. He was the first bog mummy with a beard. His hair had been cut with scissors shortly before his death and his fingernails were neatly trimmed. These things suggest that he was most likely not a laborer or a warrior. Archaeologist Anne Ross believes Lindow Man was probably a chieftain or a priest.

It was common for the ancient Celts to sacrifice humans and animals to please their gods. Many scientists believe that Lindow Man was part of one of these ancient sacrifices.

According to archaeologist Anne Ross, Lindow Man could have been sacrificed to the three Celtic gods Taranis, Esus, and Teutates. That is why he suffered from such "overkill." The god Teutates was offered his victims in pools and wells, while the victims of Esus were strangled and had their throats cut. Although those offered to Taranis were sometimes burned in wicker cages, they were also killed with weapons. Lindow Man's crushed skull shows he was also hit with some kind of club.

ARTIFACT

One of the main ingredients in a British skin cream called "Essence of Time" was peat from the Lindow Moss. The makers of this anti-aging cream bragged that it was peat that kept Lindow Man's skin "young and soft" for twenty-five hundred years!

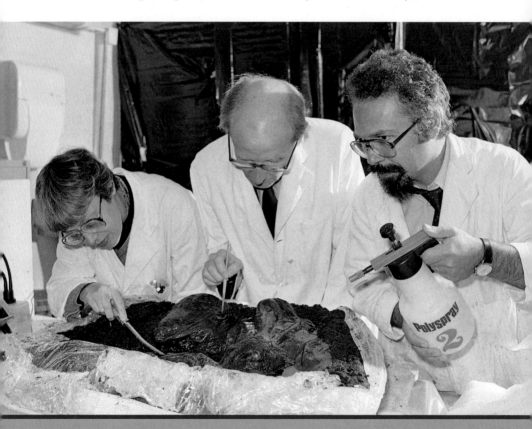

Scientists and researchers study Lindow Man at the British Museum in London, where he is now on display.

The sad and fascinating figure of Lindow Man can be visited at the British Museum in London. It is one of the museum's most popular attractions.

Mummies speak to us from the past. By studying them, scientists have learned a great deal about ancient cultures that is useful to us today.

The preserved bugs found in Egyptian mummies helped scientists understand the history of diseases in the Nile delta. The contents of mummy stomachs have taught us about ancient farming, cooking, and diet. Scientists are hopeful that the discovery of a preserved brain in the mummy of an elderly Egyptian queen will teach us about diseases in ancient times. It may even help us find a cure for a disease that makes old people lose their memories.

Without knowing it, people of ancient cultures created time capsules, or messages for the future, delivered in the preserved bodies of their dead.

We look at mummies with a strange mixture of fear, disgust, and curiosity. They hold the keys to the past and maybe the future as well.

New Words

archaeologist (ar-kee-**ol**-uh-jist) someone who studies the past by digging up old buildings and objects and examining them carefully

artificial (ar-ti-**fish**-uhl) false, not real or not natural, as in artificial flowers

bog (**bog**) an area of wet, spongy land

Bronze Age (**bronz age**) a period of history before the production of iron when bronze was used to make tools and weapons, usually dated between 3000 and 1100 B.C.

canopic jar (**kuh**-noh-pik **jar**) small decorated jars in which the Egyptians stored the organs removed from bodies during mummification

coffin (**kawf**-in) a long container into which a dead person is placed for burial

corpse (**korps**) a dead body

cultures (**kuhl**-churz) way of life, ideas, customs, and traditions of groups of people

embalmers (**em**-bahm-ers) people who treat the dead in order to prevent decay

lacquer (**lak**-ur) a liquid coating put on wood or metal to give it a shiny finish and protect it

New Words

maggots (**mag**-uhtz) larva of certain flies

manganese (**man**-guh-neez) a grayish-white metallic element

natron (**nay**-trahn) naturally occurring salt formed of sodium carbonate and sodium bicarbonate

peat (**peet**) brown, partly decayed plant matter found in bogs or swamps that can be used as fuel or compost

pharaoh (**fair**-roh) an Egyptian king

preservation (prez-ur-**va**-shuhn) keeping free from decay

resin (**rez**-in) a substance from plants and trees used for making lacquers, glue, and rubber

rituals (**rich**-oo-uhls) actions always performed in the same way as parts of religious or social ceremonies

sarcophagus (sar-**kah**-fuh-guhs) a stone container for a coffin, in Greek it means "flesh eater"

thaw (**thaw**) to become room temperature after being frozen

For Further Reading

Deem, James A. *Bodies from the Bog.* Boston: Houghton Mifflin Co., 1998.

Harris, Nathaniel. *Mummies: Very Peculiar History.* London, UK: Franklin Watts, 1995.

Malam, John. *Mummies.* Boston: Houghton Mifflin Co., 2003.

Pearson, Michael Parker, and Andrew T. Chamberlain. *Earthly Remains: The History and Science of Preserving Human Bodies.* Oxford, UK: Oxford University Press, 2002.

Pringle, Heather. *The Mummy Congress: Science, Obsession, and the Everlasting Dead.* New York: Hyperion Press, 2001.

Putnam, James. *Mummy.* Bethany, MO: Fitzgerald Books, 2001.

Organizations

American Museum of Natural History

Central Park West at 79th Street

New York, NY 10024-5192

(212) 769-5100

www.amnh.org

The Metropolitan Museum of Art

1000 Fifth Avenue at 82nd Street

New York, NY 10028-0198

(212) 535-7710

www.metmuseum.org/

Smithsonian Institution

PO Box 37012

SI Building, Room 153, MRC 010

Washington, DC 20013-7012

(202) 633-1000

www.si.edu

Resources

Web Sites

At the Tomb of Tutankhamen
www.nationalgeographic.com/egypt/
This firsthand account of the opening of King Tut's tomb transports us back in time. Photos and correspondence from this period help to complete the journey to February 1923.

Mummies of Ancient Egypt
www.si.umich.edu/CHICO/mummy/
What is a mummy? Who were the mummies? How were they made? This Web site answers all the major questions about the mummies of ancient Egypt.

Mummies of the World
www.pbs.org/wgbh/nova/peru/mummies/
PBS online provides a brief overview of the different mummies found throughout the world. Specific expeditions take a closer look at such finds as the Incan ice mummies and the Iceman.

Index

Index

About the Author

Richard Raleigh lives in Poughkeepsie, New York, with his wife and daughter. He is a folklorist and translator, as well as a professor of literature and creative writing.